THE HISPANIC SOCIETY OF AMERICA

D1320681

# HISPANIC
## NOTES & MONOGRAPHS

ESSAYS, STUDIES, AND BRIEF
BIOGRAPHIES ISSUED BY THE
HISPANIC SOCIETY OF AMERICA

## III

# BALTASAR GRACIÁN

BY

AUBREY F. G. BELL

OXFORD UNIVERSITY PRESS
HUMPHREY MILFORD
1921

PRINTED IN ENGLAND
AT THE OXFORD UNIVERSITY PRESS
BY FREDERICK HALL

## PREFACE

To look through the bibliography of any foreign literature is often a melancholy task to a patriotic Englishman, so few are the English names he finds there. Gracián is a case in point, for no English name is to be found among his critics. Yet here, as in other cases, it would be false to draw an inference of incurious apathy, since a part at least of Gracián's writings is probably known to a far larger number of readers in England than in countries which have provided specialists to dissect him and his works. With the increased interest now taken in Spanish studies in England it is, however, probable that he will soon become the object of more serious attention here. Owing to his remarkable views on progress and civilization, and his fondness for dabbling in the psychology of nations, he is perhaps of peculiar interest at the present time.

For the following lists of works I am indebted to the kindness of Professor James Fitzmaurice-Kelly. (See his *Historia de la Literatura Española*. Tercera edición, corregida. Madrid, 1921.)

MODERN EDITIONS : *El Héroe. Reimpresión de la edición de 1639.* Ed. A. Coster (Chartres, 1911); *El Héroe* and *El Discreto.* Ed. A. Farinelli (Madrid, 1900); *El Discreto, Oráculo Manual,* and *El Héroe* in *Biblioteca de Autores Españoles,* vol. lxv ; *El Criticón.* Ed. J. Cejador. 2 vols. (Madrid, 1913, 14) ; *El Héroe, El Discreto,* and *El Oráculo.* Ed. A. Reyes (Madrid, 1918) [Biblioteca Calleja] ; *Cartas inéditas.* Ed. M. Compañy in *Revista Crítica,* vol. i (1896), pp. 81-8.

WORKS OF REFERENCE : M. Menéndez y Pelayo in *Historia de las Ideas Estéticas en España,* vol. ii (1884), pp. 535-41 ; B. Croce, *I Trattatisti italiani del 'concet-*

*tismo' e Baltasar Gracian* (Napoli, 1890);
A. Farinelli in *Revista crítica*, vol. i
(1896); K. Borinski, *Baltasar Gracian
und die Hofliteratur in Deutschland* (Halle,
1894); N. J. de Liñán y Heredia, *Baltasar Gracián* (Madrid, 1902); A. Morel-
Fatio, *Cours du Collège de France, 1909–10,
sur les moralistes espagnols du XVII<sup>e</sup>
siècle et en particulier sur Baltasar Gracian*
in *Bulletin Hispanique*, vol. xii (1910),
pp. 201–4, 330–4; A. Morel-Fatio, *Liste
chronologique des lettres de Baltasar Gracian
dont l'existence a été signalée* in *Bulletin
Hispanique*, vol. xii (1910), pp. 204–6;
A. Morel-Fatio, *Gracian interprété par
Schopenhauer*, in *Bulletin Hispanique*, vol.
xii (1910), pp. 337–407; A. Coster, *Sur
une Contrefaçon de l'édition de El Héroe
de 1639*, in *Revue Hispanique*, vol. xxiii
(1910), p. 594; V. Brouillier, *Notes sur
l'Oraculo Manual* in *Bulletin Hispanique*,
vol. xiii (1911), pp. 316–36; Azorín,
pseud. [J. Martínez Ruiz], *Baltasar Gracián*
in *Lecturas Españolas* (1912), pp. 65–71;
A. Coster, *Baltasar Gracián, 1601–58*, in

*Revue Hispanique*, vol. xxix (1913), pp. 347–75² ; A. Bonilla y San Martín, *Un manuscrito inédito del siglo xvi, con dos cartas autógrafas de B. G.* in *Revista crítica hispano-americana*, vol. ii (1916), pp. 121–35 ; A. Reyes, *El Suicida* (Madrid, 1917), pp. 84–6.

# BALTASAR GRACIÁN
## (1601–1658)

### I

GRACIÁN (1) died thirteen years after
Quevedo, and eight years before the Portuguese Dom Francisco Manuel de Mello.
They are the three great prose-writers
of the Peninsula in the seventeenth century. Baltasar Jerónimo Gracián y Morales
was born on January 8, 1601, at Belmonte,
not the birthplace of Fray Luis de Leon,
but a village in the neighbourhood of
Calatayud and of Bilbilis, the birthplace
of Martial. If it be true that *bene vixit
qui bene latuit,* Gracián's life was exemplary,
since little is known about it. He appears
to have been brought up by an uncle at
Toledo, and at the age of eighteen entered

2235.3        B

the Company of Jesus. Later he taught
Scripture, the Humanities, Theology, and
Philosophy in various Jesuit colleges,
principally, perhaps, in that of Calatayud.
He evidently taught with success, and
won the respect of his superiors, for in
1642 he was promoted to become Rector
of the Jesuit College at Tarragona. From
April 1640 to July 1641 he was at Madrid,
so that he was not in Catalonia during the
war in which Tarragona was captured in
December 1640, and in which Mello took
part. He may, however, have met Mello
earlier in the year at Madrid. Unlike
Mello's, his life appears to have been
peaceful and uneventful till the year of his
death (1658). In that year the publication
of the third part (1657) of *El Criticón*
brought him into trouble with his superiors.
Although it was not published under the
author's name, it would seem that the
Provincial of the Jesuits had admonished
Gracián, after the appearance of the second
part in 1655, not to proceed with the
work. Gracián, however, who had suc-

ceeded in publishing the first two parts, and who rightly considered the third the best and the necessary crown and completion of his work, appears to have been as determined as was another Jesuit, Padre Isla, a century later, with his *Fray Gerundio*, that it should see the light without delay, or at least suffered himself to be persuaded by his friends. The Provincial, angered by this act of disobedience, publicly reprimanded Padre Gracián, inflicted on him the humiliation of fasting on bread and water, deprived him of the Chair of Scripture, and ordered him to retire to Graus (2). The General of the Order approved these severities, and further ordered that Padre Gracián's rooms should be visited from time to time, that he should be allowed to keep nothing under lock and key, and while under arrest should be denied the use of pen, ink, or paper. Gracián felt this punishment keenly, perhaps even bitterly resented it, and he requested that he might be transferred to an order of monks or mendicant friars. To this petition no answer was sent, and we know nothing more of Gracián from this time (June 1658) till his death at the little town of Tarazona on December 6.

## II

GRACIÁN was of opinion that humility was not a quality often found among Spaniards, and we may doubt whether it formed any prominent part of his own character. All those who seem fools are fools, he says, and half of those who do not, and with the best will in the world the witty and ingenious Jesuit could not number himself among them. The *sabios* are few. 'There are not four in a city. Four, say I? There are not two in a kingdom. The number of the ignorant is great, that of the foolish is infinite. He who has them on his side will be master of the whole world' (3). The crowd is wooed by the demagogues (*espantavillanos* he calls them), but it is a dangerous trade because the moods of the crowd veer like

the wind. It was not to be expected
that Gracián, who made superiority his
motto, should be attracted by democracy,
and he handles it severely in *El Criticón*.
Metternich, when asked by a frightened
Archduke what was the meaning of the
din heard through the palace windows,
answered, 'C'est ce que Messieurs les
Républicains appellent la voix de Dieu.'
Gracián had said, more bluntly: 'The
voice of God? Yes, of the god Bacchus,'
and 'Let no one in any circumstance say
that the voice of the people is the voice
of God, rather it is the voice of ignorance
and all the devils.' It is important, however, to observe that in this matter he is
no respecter of rank or class. He could
not live in Spain without realizing that an
ignorant and illiterate peasant might be
the greatest of aristocrats, with the dignity
of a king in Homer. On the other hand,
'There are', he says, 'men as common
and ignorant as their lackeys, and the
truth is that a man may be a prince, yet
if he sets himself to speak of matters

which he does not understand and to give
his opinion about that of which he has no
knowledge or concern, he at once becomes
a vulgar plebeian (*hombre vulgar y plebeyo*).
For the common crowd (*el vulgo*) is but
an assembly of presumptuous, ignorant
persons who the less they understand of
a matter the more will they talk about it ',
and they bestow their admiration and
blame without understanding or knowledge. The politic man (*el buen político*)
is careful to guide *el vulgo* whither he
wishes, and if it be asked whether there
be any who wish for the applause of the
crowd and 'care to rule the masses', the
answer is that there are many such lovers
of popularity, eager for the favour of the
mob, which they court with works coarse-
grained and superficially attractive (*obras
gruesas y plausibles*). Gracián wrote
ostensibly for a smaller circle. In the
preface to his *El Comulgatorio*, a brief
religious treatise of which any author
might well be proud, he declares that it is
the only one of his children which he

recognizes as legitimate ; that is, he admitted the authorship of his other works, but professed to be a little ashamed of them. Very different, we may be sure, would be the view of his writings expressed to his intimate friends, such as Lastanosa, the celebrated numismatist of Huesca, who published Gracián's works without his consent, although perhaps not against his will (4). He wrote for the few, but would not have been sorry that the many should applaud what he had written. His place, however, was in the study ; for him there was no pleasure like that of 'reading in a select library' (5), hungrily devouring the wise and ingenious books of all nations, or that of 'a learned and discreet conversation with three or four intelligent friends, and not more, for with more all is noise and confusion. Pleasant conversation is the feast of the understanding, the delight of the soul, the relief of the heart, the crown of learning, the life of friendship, and the noblest employment for man' (6). In this world of books Gracián's

judgements were severe. We can understand how the artificial art of Calderon or
Quevedo would appeal to him more
forcibly than the natural genius of Lope
de Vega or Cervantes. Lope de Vega,
eighteen years dead, is slighted: he is
admired by *los vulgares*; Cervantes is
obviously referred to in the remark that
the writers who had attacked the romances
of chivalry had merely replaced one fool-
ishness by another. Yet it would be a
mistake to infer that Gracián was arrogant,
conceited, and presumptuous. He left
that for the *necios*. His literary verdicts
may have been one-sided, but they had
their basis in a desire for sincerity and
directness. From the same source springs
his pessimism, a pessimism which Horace
was able to express without bitterness, but
which on the lips of a Christian has always
been regarded as something peculiarly
romantic and modern, if not as a kind of
blasphemy against progress. Gracián did
not believe in progress. Fashions in
manners and language and everything

else come and go, cycle follows cycle in action and reaction, but everything goes from bad to worse, *siempre se va todo empeorando*, and life is but a perpetual warfare, a *milicia contra malicia*. ' Tous les siècles se ressemblent par la méchanceté des hommes.' Gracián had no illusions as to a golden age. The world has always been the same : *el mismo fué siempre que es.* He saw no millennium looming ahead, and if he believed in a golden age in the past, he certainly placed it in an immeasurably remote antiquity. The pessimism which attracted Schopenhauer was thus impersonal and philosophic, and differed from that of the romantic poet or the praiser of times past. The moral philosopher is at least happy in the knowledge that, if his own age is bad, the next is likely to be worse. Gracián's pessimism really answered to a time of reaction after a period of great effort and achievement, and thus corresponds to that of Leopardi and Schopenhauer after the Napoleonic wars, and to that which inspires brilliant

treatises in the twentieth century (7).
Against this pessimism Gracián has only
to offer his theory of the heroic : eminent
men, a Michelangelo, a Titian, Góngora
or Quevedo, are not well appreciated in
their lifetime, but they begin to live when
they die ; and those who would win their
way into the heart of immortality must be
soldiers on earth, taking for their watch-
words high virtue and heroic valour, and
ever perfecting themselves in the light of
an ideal which may not, indeed cannot be
understood by the world. Gracián had
no belief in the progress and gradual perfection of the human race, but in every
age a few individuals might reasonably
aspire to greatness.

### III

AMONG Gracián's modern traits is his delight in psychological analysis. He studies men, both as individuals and in groups and nations. His remarks on the various countries of Europe betray much acuteness and careful observation. Outside Spain his preference is for Portugal, while France and Germany are judged the most unfavourably. He seems to have been greatly struck by the appearance of the English. They are as fair of body as ugly of soul (heretics). Spain has riches, France numbers, England beauty. The face of Europe is fair in England, grave in Spain, spirited in France, discreet in Italy, cool in Germany, fringed with curls in Sweden, placid in Poland, effeminate in Greece, and frowning in Muscovy. When the good things of the world were divided honour went to the Spanish, profit to the French, good taste to the English, and authority to the Italians. When Valour bequeathed his body to the world, having nothing else to leave in his will, the Italians had the head, the French the hands and arms (although the Genoese stole the nails), the Venetians the cheeks, the Sicilians the tongue. To the Irish went the liver (*higado* = courage), to the Germans the waist, to the Chinese the back. The Japanese, who are 'the Spanish of Asia', and are characterized by a certain temerity, received the heart, the Swedes the breast, the Turks the legs. The Spanish arrived late, and since there were not two hearts they are doomed to obtain whatever they can wrench from other nations, an arrangement which suits them excellently. As to the English, 'I leave', says Valour, 'to the English my face. You shall be beautiful as angels, but I fear lest, like fair courtesans, you may be too gracious towards Calvin and Luther

and the Devil.   Beware above all that
the fox see you not, for he will say straight-
way : "A fair exterior but no brains !"'
In the Cage of All Men the English are
in a very merry section, as being *vanos*
(vain, empty), which is 'the defect of
beauty'.   Yet elsewhere these *desvanecidos*
are spoken of as 'the most prudent English
nation'.   In England one must beware
of *perfidias* (was it from Gracián that
Napoleon derived his idea of *perfide
Albion* ?) as one must guard against
maliciousness in Spain, meanness in
France, vulgarity in Germany, and trickery
in Italy.

Gracián's analysis of Spain entails, as
must ever be the case, division into
regions.   The Andalusians talk much and
do little, the Aragonese are prudent but
dense and obstinate, the Valencians fickle,
the Galicians spiritless, the Navarrese
quick to take offence, the Catalans are
good friends of their friends, the men of
Estremadura and La Mancha are brave,
the Castilians generous, even lavish,

haughty, honourable (*hombres de bien*) and, above all, *sustanciales*. The last epithet must not be taken to mean materialist: rather it implies a Greek sense of proportion, with a splendid solidity added. Of Spain, taken as a whole, the chief characteristic is pride and magnificence. Pride and presumption dwell there among nobles and peasants alike. They are *ostentosos por naturaleza, ostentosos por superioridad.* Their houses have many coats of arms on their walls, but not a penny within. There is no common people (*vulgo*) in Spain as in other nations. They do not stoop to industry. Accordingly Spain 'is to-day as God made her, her inhabitants have done nothing to improve her, apart from the little accomplished by the Romans. Her mountains are proud and untamed as at the beginning, her innavigable rivers follow their natural course, their water has not been canalized to make fertile the desert places, the land is untilled, and industry has achieved nothing.' The dryness of the climate breeds in the

Spaniards a melancholy gravity. It is
a mountainous and therefore unproductive
country, but healthy. Its inhabitants
have extraordinary virtues and vices. They
are very spirited (*bizarros*), even haughty
and impatient. They are rather sensible
than ingenious ; brave but slow ; generous,
sober in eating and drinking, not in dress ;
they are not very patriotic, and improve
when transplanted. They are reasonable,
but somewhat obstinate, not very devout,
but devoted to their religion. Gracián
approves the Spanish *tardanza* (*harto
presto si harto bien*) as compared with the
French impetuosity. These two nations
are fundamentally opposed to one another
in dress, food, walking and talking, character and talents, and 'a Frenchman
grafted on a Spaniard is the worst blend
of all'. The French are gay, nimble,
restless ; they do not write as they speak,
nor act as they say, and for love of money
they will undertake the vilest offices and
hire themselves out as slaves. Do they
not walk barefoot with their shoes under

their arm ? Do they not degrade themselves by permitting themselves to whistle ?
France is full of people but not of men ;
the French are industrious but mechanical,
warlike and spirited but unquiet, ingenious but superficial. They go from
extreme to extreme, and are in fact the
antipodes of the Spanish. (Yet Spain is
only now beginning to emerge from the
legend of extremes—cruelty, fanaticism,
obscurantism, and other exaggerations—
which the ignorance rather than the ill-
will of Europe has cast over the tem-
perate, sensible, and practical character of
the majority of Spaniards.) The Italians
are less abject than the French, less
haughty than the Spanish. They are
sagacious and can govern. They have
more sense than the French, and are equal
to the Spanish in natural talent. Had
the Indies been theirs, to what excellent
use they would have put them ! But they
are given to wiles and deceit. The Portuguese come best out of all these odious
comparisons. You will never find a Portu-

2285·3

C

guese who is either a fool or a coward,
two clear proofs of their descent from
Ulysses, and if they hyperbolically exalt
their own deeds and their country, and
can never forget the victorious bakeress
of Aljubarrota, they may justly claim that
there must be some smoke where there is
much fire. They are fond of music,
sensible, courtly, talented, intelligent, con-
tented with themselves, and full of admiration for the world in general. The Germans are thick of speech, vulgar, slovenly,
gluttonous. Some of them, it is true, have
been drunk but once ; in their case, however, the drunkenness lasted a lifetime.
For every Spaniard drunk you will see a
hundred Frenchmen and four hundred
Germans. You will as easily discover a
humble Spaniard or a grave and tranquil
Frenchman as an abstemious German.
The abundance of her resources only
serves to minister to furious Germany's
ceaseless wars. They are the largest, but
not the greatest men in Europe. They
have little heart and no soul, great strength

but no spirit. Their language is ancient but barbarous, and if they have skilled artificers, they have no eminent men of learning. Gracián, although subtle in many of these remarks, does not always succeed in his psychological epigrams, and like all generalizations about peoples, they are often both true and false ; but from time to time he hits off a whole nation admirably in a single phrase.

## IV

THE first published work of Gracián was *El Héroe* (1637) (8), and it was fitting that this should be so since his conception of the heroic and the superior runs through all his work—even *El Arte de Ingenio* has a chapter headed *De los dichos heróicos*. *El Héroe*, in twenty short chapters, called *primores*, deals with all greatness, but is chiefly occupied with heroes in the more ordinary sense. Gracián professes to despise the vulgar herd, *profanum vulgus*, but with some inconsistency he devotes much attention to it. Some men, he says, and not the least wise, prefer the admiration of a few to the applause of a multitude ; yet he advises his hero to be ' plausible ', that is to woo the crowd, ' since the gentleness of a plausible speech

flatters the ear, whereas the dryness of a
metaphysical idea tortures and vexes it',
and he will really always have one eye on
appearances. Eminence is not enough
without the art of winning esteem, and the
hero will be wise to throw a sop to the
envious *criticismo* of Spain and commit
some foolish action of trivial import in
order not to appear too perfect. It may
be objected that perfection rarely descends
from Heaven in human form, and when
it is realized what greatness requires of its
votary, it will be seen that comparatively few
persons will have to resort to this ' ring of
Polycrates' policy. A bold magnificence,
a natural superiority, and a sublime sympathy are among the hero's most useful
gifts. He must be large-hearted, must
emulate great men of the past, must excel,
'since many mediocrities do not make
one greatness', choosing, if possible, an
untrodden path. He must accurately
gauge his fortune, so as to be able to leave
it before it leaves him, must never lay
claim to great gifts, always have the

artifice to hide all artifice, and must train his taste to a severe and critical difficulty of satisfaction, since 'he who praises over-much mocks either himself or others'. He must unite acuteness with courage, industry with natural talent, intelligence with will-power; he must dominate or dis-semble his desires, must be master of himself and so of everything, must dis-cover and develop his true bent, and, above all, a thought constantly recurring under various guises, he must hold himself and his faculties in reserve, and must know how to renew his greatness. Lastly, and as if by an afterthought, he is reminded that greatness is based upon virtue, and that to be a hero of the world is little or nothing, but to be a hero of Heaven is much. The work is illustrated by a few historical anecdotes, told with clearness and point, such as that of the Portuguese jeweller and Philip II, or of the King and Diego Pérez de Vargas.

*El Político D. Fernando el Católico* (1640) gives, in the career and character

of the husband of Isabella the Catholic,
Gracián's ideal of the perfect and absolute
prince, with many comments and illustra-
tions from ancient and modern history.
An index of the work would be almost as
long as the work itself. It opens with
Romulus and others on the plea that the
deeds of founders are usually prodigious,
and ends with a formidable catalogue of
eminent princes, Manuel I of Portugal
cheek by jowl with the Antonines, Charles V
jostled by Moslem rulers. This extension
is necessarily made at the expense of
depth, and despite some acute remarks
the treatise tantalizes rather than satisfies
the reader.

Gracián's next published work was a
long book entitled *Arte de Ingenio, Tratado
de Agudeza* (1642) (9). It consists of
sixty-three 'discourses', and contains the
literary theory of the *conceptistas*, explaining
'all the modes and differences of concepts'.
It is illustrated with a wealth of interesting
quotations from Spanish, Latin, Portuguese, and Italian poets. It is in this

extraordinary work, very unjustly neglected
in spite of its many absurdities, that
Gracián says : 'What culture can equal a
natural eloquence? In describing things
beautiful in themselves true art consists
in shunning art and artifice.' Unfortu-
nately to the human mind things rarely
appear beautiful in themselves. Men's
senses become dull, and it requires an
Andrenio fresh from his cave to perceive
the full beauty of the universe. Most
men have to compare, relate, harmonize
one thing with another. To this intent
intelligence without ingenuity and wit is
like the sun without rays or light ; excellent in itself, possibly, but useless for the
purposes of the world. Gracián can thus
agree with the *culteranos* that a certain
artifice is necessary to attract and enchain
the attention, but whereas they would be
content with hollow ingenuities and common metaphors, Gracián demands the
more difficult process of clothing cleverly
in words a pre-existing idea (or what
Menéndez y Pelayo called *el refinamiento*

*de la abstracción*). *Agudeza* is the link
between pure mind and the objects, it
mints abstract intelligence into useful
currency, and harmoniously interrelates
two or more objects. It may take many
forms, and even plays on words are not
forbidden, provided that they have a
foundation of thought. (*Discurso* 31 deals
with *agudeza nominal*, and one of the
instances given is *Di Ana eres Diana*.)
What, he asks, would Augustine be without his subtleties, Ambrose without his
emphasis, Martial without his wit, Horace
without his maxims? Without the inspira-
tion of wit (*sin alma de agudeza*) *culteranismo* is 'a tedious, empty, useless affecta-
tion', and the well-worn metaphors of sun,
eagle, flower, vulgar ineptitudes; he condemns the preachers who abandon the
substance of the Scriptures for cold allegories and hackneyed metaphors. Gracián
will have antitheses, paradoxes, and metaphors in plenty, but he insists that they
should be not dry sticks, but the natural-
unnatural growth of the tree of thought.

One cannot help suspecting that he was anxious to find an excuse for his own evident delight in juggling with words. It was a dangerous theory, since even the talented Gracián could not always infuse thought into verbal affectations, and when the current fails his ingenuities become as barren and insipid as those of the *culteranos* whom he condemned.

*El Discreto* (1646) is not a mere repetition of *El Héroe*, although it resembles it in many of its precepts. The *Héroe* embraces all eminence and the *Discreto* is a figure 'non seulement de l'homme ingénieux et fin, ou de l'homme avisé et prudent, mais d'un composé de tout ce qui fait l'*honnête homme* de l'époque' (10); and the first French translator was not misleading when he adopted as his title *L'Homme Universel* (Paris, 1727). *L'Honneste Homme* (1630) is the title of a work by Nicolas Faret, which may have influenced Gracián considerably, especially as it was translated into Spanish by Ambrosio de Salazar in

1633. The 'discreet' man must have both *genio* and *ingenio* ; in other words, it is not enough to possess great gifts, one must know how to use and apply them (intelligence without *agudeza* is a rayless sun). Intelligence and diligence together are all-powerful. The diligence will consist in adapting the intelligence. The importance of manner is very great. One man will offend with the identical words with which another succeeds in flattering. There is room for *aliño* (order, ornament) even in holiness. The discreet man will not be unequal, but superior to moods and humours and consistently moderate and prudent, yet versatile, adaptable, rather grave than given to mockery, although the gravest should have a quaint spice of wit (*un grano de donosura*). He may be as perfect as he like, but should not show more than one half of his perfection to the world ; he must know how to wait, how to retire, how to impose himself by natural or artificial superiority. He must be courtly and magnificent, turning even disadvantages to his own use. The whole art of life consists in choice, nor is it a vulgar art to know how to make the most of things (*gozar de las cosas*). He must distinguish clearly between the falsely (*hazañero*) and truly (*hazañoso*) heroic : Caligula and Nero but not Julius Caesar might triumph for having slain a wild boar. He must avoid the paradoxical, fantastic, and extravagant, and realize that ' a useless curiosity is worse than idleness '. He will divide his life into three parts : in the first he converses with the dead (reading); in the second with the living (travelling); in the third with himself (meditation). The work is composed of somewhat disconnected chapters : essays, dialogues, fables (those of the peacock and of the ass and Fortune are most elaborately developed).

For long Gracián owed his European fame principally to his *Oráculo Manual y Arte de Prudencia* (1647) (11), which Menéndez y Pelayo described as ' the most confusing and difficult work in the

Spanish language'. To the interest taken by Schopenhauer in this work (his translation was published posthumously at Leipzig in 1862) was primarily due the modern research concerning Gracián's life and works which has borne good fruit in the treatises of Karl Borinski in Germany, Signor Benedetto Croce and Signor Arturo Farinelli in Italy, and M. Alfred Morel-Fatio and M. Adolphe Coster in France. M. Morel-Fatio has shown that Schopenhauer's version is far from flawless, and has emphasized the need of caution in translating an author who gives an esoteric meaning to some of his words. The difficult confusion of the *Oráculo* is increased by the fact that its three hundred maxims are ill arranged and contain some repetitions, while many of them can be better understood by reference to the chapters of *El Héroe* and *El Discreto* from which they are derived. Others may have been taken from lost works by Gracián entitled *El Varón Atento* and *El Galante* (if these

books were ever written). The *Oráculo*
is in fact a summary, somewhat loosely
put together and occasionally contra-
dictory. For instance, the prudent man
is to be commonplace in nothing (*en nada
vulgar*); he should not make himself too
easily intelligible, since men admire what
they do not understand ; he is to be vexed
if his words and deeds (*sus cosas*) please
all men, for this is a sure sign of their
little worth ; yet he is exhorted to talk to
all men in their language, to speak with
the voice of common folly in the market-
place (12), and not to be alone in con-
demning what pleases the many. The
only means of being popular is to don the
skin of the ass. He is to avoid familiarity
(*excusar llaneza de trato*), yet adapt himself to all men (*hacerse a todos*). He is to
be superior, *singular*, yet we are told,
almost in the words of Santa Teresa, that
singularity 'is always hateful', 'is always
condemned', 'is to condemn others'.
But one must remember that there is an
element of paradox in all things, and that

an inevitable dualism runs through all
Gracián's work : that of the pure idea and
of its application in the world. The need
of *genio* and *ingenio* and of reservation
are expounded at the very outset of the
*Oráculo*. One should have an ideal but
adapt oneself to circumstances. Never
lay all your cards on the table nor make
known your desires, since they will meet
with opposition or flattery, and the crushed
orange changes from gold to mud (*no
descubrir toda su perfección de una vez ;
llevar sus cosas con suspensión*). Yet while
keeping his inner perfection unspotted
from the world, the prudent man will
develop it diligently in secret. He must
realize his true vocation and learn from
experience. ' All men make mistakes, but
the wise man conceals his past errors,
and the fool those which he is about to
commit.' (On this principle the sixteenth-
century Spanish judge had the old men
executed for their crimes and the young
for the crimes of which they would have
been guilty had they lived.) Talent with-

out diligence will avail little and 'mediocrity with application attains more than superiority without'. Some of the maxims are excellent, as 'All that is natural has always been more pleasing than the artificial', 'A grain of good sense is worth more than tons of subtlety', 'Continual wit is a serious defect', 'One should not become paradoxical in order to avoid the commonplace'; and Gracián's readers may regret that he did not always follow them. Others have a casuistic and indeed a cynical character, although some of them appear more so at first sight than they may prove on closer inspection or by comparison with parallel passages. The prudent man in his dealings with the world is certainly an opportunist and masquerades as a fox when he cannot masquerade as a lion. What causes good will he is to do himself, but what evokes hatred he carries out through another. He must not inflict *irreparable* harm on others for his own benefit, but he will shun the unfortunate, although always willing to share his own misfortunes, since 'solitude doubles and makes them intolerable'. He will think with the few and vote with the many, and will make a virtue of dissimulation. It is therefore with something of a shock that one finds in the last maxim of all the brief exhortation 'and in a word, holy'. The preceding precepts might make an accomplished man of the world, but would scarcely conduce to any but a very abstract saintliness. Involuntarily one is reminded of the *diligencia*-driver who, after crawling many a weary league, whips up his horses to enter the town in fine style at the end of the journey. The *Oráculo* contains much ingenuity and some real thought, and, although it has been excessively praised, is far from deserving to be cast aside as a mere essay in obscurity or as a string of commonplaces dressed up in the meretricious plumes of paradox. *El Comulgatorio* (1555) (13) appeared between the second and third parts of *El Criticón*, as though to propitiate Gracián's ecclesiastical censors. It consists of fifty brief meditations founded on passages of the Old and New Testament as a preparation for the Holy Communion. It is excellent in matter and style, and the author's restraint is shown by the fact that even in dealing with the subject of Martha and Mary he refrains from antithesis. Besides these prose works, a poem entitled *Selvas del Año* (1668) is ascribed to Gracián. If it be his, it only shows that, like Quevedo and Mello, he was no poet, and that poetry is more dependent than prose on a touch of nature, and may be killed by artifice—of thought (*conceptismo*) or verbal (*culteranismo*).

V

THE essence of Gracián may be contained in the *Oráculo Manual*, but his longest and his best work is *El Criticón* (1651–7) (14), and it is this which will always be most widely read and on which his fame will ultimately rest. By comparison with the *Oráculo* it makes very easy reading, its style is simple and straightforward, with a conciseness which is rarely allowed to border on obscurity. It is the life history of two friends, Critilo and Andrenio, who are also father and son. Andrenio is suckled by a wild beast and brought up in an inaccessible cave on a small island (St. Helena). The earth quakes and he finds himself free, and sees for the first time 'the greatness, beauty, harmony, strength and variety of the created world', which custom stales to our senses. He watches the sun rise and set, night with her train of stars and the white majesty of the moon ; he sees the earth arrayed in fruits and flowers and a diversity of creatures, the miracle of the rain, the sea with the continual yet barren progress of its waves. The career of shipwrecked Critilo has been less happy. Born among men, at sea, and brought up at Goa, where his betrothed Felisinda was snatched from him almost at the last moment by her ambitious parents and taken to Spain, he has found that *homo homini lupus*, and when from their island they see ships approaching in the distance, he warns Andrenio against placing his trust in man. Men are very bad indeed, he says; but women are worse. They arrive in Spain, and the first thing they see is a host of children fondled by a gracious lady till they are devoured by wild beasts to which she treacherously lures them, only a few being saved by a second lady who appears crowned with light. This is an allegory of the souls of men torn by desires in their youth under the guidance of their natural inclination, which destroys most of them before they can be saved by Reason. The two friends go searching for men and meet a centaur who tells them that the race of eminent men in arms and letters is perishing, and bids them, sarcastically but indeed prophetically, look for modern heroes in the air (men of vain presumption). He leads them to the principal square of a city, which they find full not of men but of lions, tigers, leopards, basilisks, wolves, bulls, panthers, many foxes, serpents, dragons. Here presents go to the rich, the poor are neglected, the wise are despised, the foolish and ignorant are placed in authority, the wicked are exalted, the good abased. Falsehood is held in high honour, but Truth is beaten and cast out. A judge condemns a mosquito to be drawn and quartered, but takes off his hat to a criminal elephant. The soldiers prolong war as being their livelihood. They now continue their journey, but meet

False Appearances in a carriage drawn by
serpents and driven by a fox, and they are
given a lift and taken out of the straight
and narrow path to the fountain of deceit.
They presently reach a great city con-
taining a perfect labyrinth of streets.
Andrenio loses his head among its plea-
sures, but Critilo goes to the court of the
learned and discreet Queen Artemia, who
sends an old man to rescue Andrenio
from the city of King Fraud, and they
return to the palace of Artemia, where the
time is spent in philosophical discussions.
King Fraud or Falimundo sends Envy,
Flattery, and Malice to stir up the people
against Queen Artemia. She hesitates
where to take refuge and finally decides
in favour of Toledo, which made even
Queen Isabella the Catholic afraid of
being less discreet than its inhabitants,
and which had increased in excellence
since neighbouring Madrid had drawn off
its dregs. Critilo and Andrenio take
leave of her and go towards Madrid. On
the road they are taken prisoners by a fair

lady (Delight) with a crowd of other persons of all degrees, bound by desires, and are taken to the Inn of the World. This has a magnificent front entrance, but its back is miserable and gloomy. Critilo who, unlike Andrenio, went round to look at the back, succeeds in rescuing his friend from this dangerous abode, into which men go singing and come out in tears. They at length reach Madrid, where they are taken in, literally and metaphorically, by the enchantress Falsirena. With the assistance of Egenio, the man with six senses, Critilo searches for Andrenio, whom Falsirena has carried off while Critilo was away on an excursion to visit the Escorial. They hunt for him through the capital and court. They find beasts of burden, laden with silver and gold, parrots, dogs, monkeys, and other victims of modern Circes. When they have at last discovered and set free Andrenio, the three proceed to the great Fair of the World and examine its wares, such as silence, experience, and patience.

## VI

In Part II (1653) Critilo and Andrenio
are advancing up the hill of life, in the
autumn of man's age. They meet hundred-
eyed Argus. They find shade and refresh-
ment by the way, furnished by Plato,
Seneca, and other wise men of old. They
arrive at the large custom-house of life,
where all are examined before being admitted to manhood. Some are here severely
reprimanded for having books of poetry
and novels, and one is even caught in
possession of a romance of chivalry. They
ask if they may read the authors who had
written against these books, but Prudence
answers that in no wise shall this be
permitted since these reformers had only
substituted one folly for another. Cards
and whistling, good only for the French,

are also sternly forbidden, but one may
listen to a Portuguese playing the guitar
so long as one does not play it oneself.
Argus then conducts them to a pass from
which all life is seen outspread, the world
from end to end and all the centuries.
Thence they descry Rome and Venice,
Toledo, which looks as if it were threaten-
ing the heavens, the palace of the Louvre
(*Lobero*) and other famous places.  They
then visit the palace of the discreet
Salastano, a great collector of records
and relics of heroes and celebrities.  They
now cross the Pyrenees into France, and
by means of a golden club, more effi-
cacious than Hercules's club of wood,
succeed in entering the City of Gold.
They soon escape from its snares and go
to the gleaming palace of the wise Queen
Sofisbella.  Here various poets and
historians and moral philosophers, beginning with Seneca, are discussed; but
while Critilo is examining the treasures of
learning, Andrenio takes the path of folly
and visits the Square of the Common

People, where there is much talk in
default of knowledge. The description
has a singularly modern air. Andrenio becomes quite indignant and asks why these
ignorant clod-hoppers should concern
themselves with matters about which they
know nothing. 'They came upon a group
which was governing the world. One was
devising ways and means, another was
publishing decrees ; they fostered trade,
they reduced expenditure. "This," said
Andrenio, "must be the Parliament, it
can't be anything else, just listen how
they talk." "What they chiefly lack,"
said the Wise Man, "is good sense. They
are all men who after mismanaging their
private affairs attempt to manage affairs of
State." "Miserable *canaille*," exclaimed
Andrenio. "How came they to meddle
in the art of governing?" "Here, you
see," said the Serpent Man, "all air their
opinions" (*dan su voto*),' although, as the
Wise Man says thoughtfully, they seem to
know more of the *bota* than of the *voto*,
to have more spirit than sense (15). There

were many other groups, in which all were
grumbling about the Government. Critilo
meanwhile has arrived at the glass steps
of the palace of Fortune. The first step
is the difficulty, and it is only mounted by
the help of Favour, who extends his hand
to the ignorant, fraudulent, liars, and
flatterers. But Andrenio is discovered
to be already on the top of the steps and
he gives a helping hand to the less fortu-
nate Critilo. They find Fortune not blind
but grave and serene, with piercing eyes.
She defends herself from the world's accu-
sation of blindly scattering her gifts. The
simple truth is that her hands are not her
own. They belong to two princes, of
Church and State. She summons Money,
Posts, and Honours, and they excuse
themselves by pointing out that the un-
deserving have a hundred ways of winning
them which are denied to the virtuous.
Fortune then shows that her gifts, in all
their apparent injustice, are most accurately weighed in the balance of her
attendant Equity, so that, for instance,

those in high honour are full of care, and
those who have the advantage of letters
have the compensating disadvantage of
poverty.   Critilo and Andrenio, however,
are saved by good luck (Ventura) from
becoming the victims of Fortune, and
cross by a drawbridge leading from Fortune to Virtue.   But a false hermit warns
them that they will not find access to the
palace of Queen Virtelia an easy matter,
and advises them to take a short cut, a
path leading to a no less powerful Queen,
very like Virtelia.   He guides them to the
convent of Hipocrinda, where the most
ravening wolves have the most pleasant
fleeces.   Critilo, however, inquires awk-
wardly for True Happiness, and they
leave the convent and equip themselves
for their more arduous way in a great
armoury filled with the weapons of heroes
of all nations.   They arrive at the Palace
of the Soul, built for virtue, inhabited by
vice, fair to look upon and full of iniquity.
A satyr leads them to the door ; false
courtesy, the ruin of thousands, bids them

enter. They examine various follies and vices and make the acquaintance of the World, the Flesh, and the Devil. They leave them there disputing and begin the ascent, guided by a man of light. After many difficulties and dangers of wild beasts, they come in sight of the palace of Virtue, but to their disappointment find that it is not shining with jewels but built of dull grey stone. It is guarded against all comers by two giants of pride, but humbling themselves, the pilgrims creep in past the giants' feet. They inquire for the virtues, but find that Justice is in some one else's house (*justicia y no en mi casa*), Truth away with the children, and so with the rest, but in the centre of the house they discover seated on a throne the perfect beauty of Virtelia. She is giving audience to her many suitors—a crooked mother who would teach her daughter to walk straight, a fastidious lady who wishes to go to heaven if there is a special road thither for ladies, a prince desirous of virtues so long as they are not those of

the common people. Virtelia asks him
if he wishes to go to the same heaven as
others, and he answers, after some hesita-
tion : yes, if there is no other. Virtue
being its own reward, Virtelia embraces
Critilo and Andrenio, but since virtue is
never stagnant, but always flowing and
progressive, they are sent on in search of
Felisinda. They now come to a bridge
leading to the city of worldly honour
(Honoria). It is strewn with ' buts ' and
' if nots ' (16) over which most persons are
tripped up and fall into the river of
laughter. The two friends cross by
cleverly imitating a blind and deaf man,
and enter a city of magnificent palaces,
few of whose roofs of glass are, however,
whole, having been shattered by stones
flung by Momus or gossip. The famous
*honra, punto de honra, negra honrilla* is
discussed. One is reminded that in the
sixteenth century one Spanish soldier is
said to have stabbed another for being
unfaithful to his wife—the wife of the
stabber. After realizing how great are

the efforts required to scale the heights
of worldly honour and their insecurity,
Critilo is inclined to renounce them as
sour grapes, but they are helped up by
a wonderful shadow. They come to a
fountain, after drinking of which the ambitious forget their friends. After narrowly
escaping from the terrible monster Envy,
they watch the world's innumerable mad-
men in their several cages, and only escape
being lynched by them owing to a friendly
giant blowing a powerful blast on the horn
of Truth, whereupon the crowd of their
persecutors turn tail and flee.

## VII

THE two pilgrims at length in part III (1657) approach the ruinous palace of Old Age (Vegecia), into which the vigilant porters receive Andrenio by the door of horrors and Critilo by the door of honours. Later they come to the Cave of Pleasure in which men try to drown old age. Here (they are now in Germany) wine reigns supreme and gives birth to heresy, slander, avarice, envy, and other evils. On their way to the Kingdom of Truth they are met by a multitude fleeing, but push forward and enter the kingdom. When, however, Truth gives birth to a son (Hatred), even Critilo is carried away in the general stampede. They spend much time in listening to Disillusion deciphering the world's paradoxes and sophistries. They are discussing the world and its ways when

Andrenio is carried off by a centaur to a doorless palace in which men mostly become invisible in the sense that they throw stones and conceal the hand that threw them or compose verses for others to recite. Critilo penetrates into the palace by the help of a keen-sighted, hundred-eyed friend, who lets in a ray of light: the palace vanishes, and Andrenio and Critilo set out for the Court of Wisdom, the former adopting the simplicity of a dove, the latter the cunning of a serpent. They can only reach their destination, however, when they allow their two extremes to meet. They come upon a crier forbidding or ingeniously modifying many proverbs (some sixty examples are given). They then proceed towards Rome and Felisinda and discover two men fighting, and, moreover, that they themselves are the subject of their quarrel, one of the men wishing to guide them to the region of light and immortality, the other to the region of quietness and rest. They choose the former and

2285.3          E.

find a palace in which Pride reigns, with presumption, ceremony, and sloth. They next come to the Cave of Nothingness, into which pours a stream of cities, courts, and kingdoms, palaces, books, many great men, beauty, nobility, helped into the dreadful cave by sloth and vice. Among the books thrown in are cold novels, fantastic dreams, bad plays, and the majority of the Spanish historians, held unworthy of the heroic deeds of Spain. They now arrive at Rome, and after a discussion on the nature of happiness are informed that Felisinda, wife of Critilo and mother of Andrenio, is no longer on earth, but that they will find her in heaven if they know how to deserve such a reward by their conduct in their earthly pilgrimage. From the highest of the seven hills of Rome they are shown the whole world and all that has ever happened or ever will happen, the future being but a reflection and repetition of the past. The world's fashions pass before them, those of dress, language, and others, in all their changing absurdity.

Lodged at the Inn of Life, they notice that although their hostess is fair, pleasant, and attentive, the guests go disappearing in a mysterious way. Raising one of the tiles of the pavement, they discover a great cellar in which all the guests are lying dead. Death comes and explains and excuses her methods. She is forced to proceed unsystematically, so that no one among fault-finding mortals should be able to complain. Critilo and Andrenio are about to be seized when they discover that there exists a remedy even against death, since 'heroes and eminent men are undying and eternal'. They are accordingly transferred to the Island of Immortality. On its precipitous cliffs many suffer shipwreck. Thus Henry VIII of England was shattered on the rock of heresy, and many writers failed to effect a landing owing to having published too much or owing to the indiscreet zeal of their admirers after their death. For the same reason the Spanish Cid, French Roland ,and Portuguese Nuno Alvarez,

although they dwell in the island, are fain
to cover their faces with their hands. The
best passports are the sweat of heroes and
the midnight oil. The two pilgrims succeed in entering, but if any wish to know
what they found there, he must take the
road of virtue and heroic valour.

Such is the framework of this remarkable and instructive work, this Spanish
*Pilgrim's Progress* completed twenty-one
years before the first edition (1678) of
Bunyan's book. It is filled in with a
host of ingenious observations and striking
phrases, and if its philosophy is not as
profound as the author or one or two of
his more fervent admirers might claim, it
certainly contains more of interesting and
skilfully presented matter than those who
have not read it would imagine. The
style is only occasionally *culterano*. As
a rule he resists the temptation to indulge
in such sentences as the following (in
Part III) : 'todo se lo lleva el viento : el
agua que fué y el vino que vino ; el sol
no es solo ni la luna es una,' but phrases

such as *tantos y tontos, cargo y carga* will occur, phrases usually, it will be noticed, full of thought. His vocabulary is pure and extensive, his sentences brief, vigorous, and without false rhetoric. The work grows in interest and unity, and he is justified in his claim to have made the second part better (less bad, he modestly says) than the first, and the third better than the second. As a whole the work must ever be regarded as one of the masterpieces of Spanish literature.

## VIII

IN reading Gracián one realizes how Spanish was Seneca. Both are less remarkable, perhaps, for what they say than for their manner of saying it, less at least for a systematized philosophy than for disconnected maxims ; both have a turn for smart and epigrammatic sentences, both are interested principally in the study of man and in moral philosophy. In Spain it has always been the personal element that counts, and this is seen clearly throughout her literature and art. Her writers have been concerned less with describing an ideal, or even with justifying the ways of God to man, than with describing man and defining his conduct towards his fellows. A strain of didacticism runs through a great part of Spanish literature. Even the picaresque novels were not exempt, and Mateo Alemán filled his *Guzmán de Alfarache* (1599) with moralizings which might not excuse, but certainly detract from the interest of his hero. Gracián was above all a moral philosopher, and the ancient writer to whom he most often refers is his fellow-countryman Seneca. The discreet man in the first part of his life will devote himself chiefly to the study of moral philosophy, of Seneca, of 'the divine Plato', and to constant reading of the Scriptures. Gracián himself owed much to the study of books, 'food of the soul, delight of the spirit', as he calls them. Among ancient writers, after Seneca, he was most influenced perhaps by Plato, from whose 'ideas' he seems to have derived the dualism which marks his doctrine, the perfect *concepto* standing apart from and requiring to be brought into connexion with them and the world. Of Spanish writers closer to his own time, he was not only or mainly influenced by religious authors, but (being, like Cervantes, an omnivorous reader) by philosophers and moralists, and he could appreciate the direct style of picaresque writings.

He must have studied Juan Luis Vives (1492–1540), who held that 'the people is a grand master in teaching how to err' and that 'the opinions of the crowd are harmful because its judgement of things is exceedingly absurd', and other philosophic writers who wrote in Latin in the sixteenth century, such as Sebastián Fox Morcillo and Francisco Sanchez. He owed something, no doubt, among others, to Benito Arias Montano in his *Instrucción de Príncipes*, to Pedro de Rivadeneyra in his *Tratado de la Religion y Virtudes que deue tener el Príncipe Christiano* (1595), to the exclusively religious writer Juan Marquez in his *El Governador Christiano* (1612), to Antonio de Guevara in his *Relox de Príncipes* (1529), to Juan Huarte de Sant Juan's *Examen de Ingenios* (1575), in its psychology and in its poor opinion of women. He gleaned something from Mateo Alemán, from *La Celestina*, which he mentions, and from Cervantes, whom he affected to despise. Above all he was influenced by Saavedra

Faxardo (1584–1648) and by Quevedo
(1580–1645). Saavedra Faxardo's *Idea de
un Príncipe Político Cristiano* was dedicated to the Prince Baltasar Carlos, to
whom Gracián likewise dedicated his
*Arte de Ingenio* and *El Discreto*, and who
died at the age of seventeen in 1646;
not, however, before he had received a
splendid immortality at the hands of
Velázquez. (Gracián mentions Velázquez
as *the* modern painter, worthy to rank
with Timanthes among the ancients:
strange, indeed, that he should give the
palm to the *llaneza* of Velázquez rather
than to the *agudeza* of El Greco.) When
Saavedra Faxardo declares (*Empresa* 74)
that man is 'the most unjust of all the
animals', we feel that he is a writer after
Gracián's heart, and Gracián no doubt
derived from him his interest in the
psychology of nations (17). The influence of Quevedo is obvious, and it was
perhaps to put himself as much as his
reader on guard that he spoke of him as
rather a mirth-provoking than a profitable

writer.   In his literary criticisms Gracián
looks principally to the moral philosophy
of the contents and to the artifice of the
style.   For him Góngora would have been
a far greater poet had he not lacked *la
moral enseñanza*, and Ariosto would have
been as great as Homer had he, like the
Greek poet, cultivated 'moral allegories'.
Gracián could not but feel the spell of the
concise and pregnant intensity of Dante,
Alighieri Alígero, to whom, indeed, he
perhaps owed as much as to Tacitus and
Martial.   Petrarca he considers whitest
ivory but cold, Tasso is a Christian Virgil.
He had probably read Castiglione's *Il
Cortegiano* {1528), both in the original
and in Boscán's celebrated translation,
and he knew the 'false aphorisms', as he
terms them, of Machiavelli (1469–1527).
He greatly admired the scholarly Traiano
Boccalini (1556–1613), 'el que más bien
supo decir mal' (he opposed the Spanish
rule in Italy), and the Piedmontese political writer Giovanni Botero (1540–1617).
Among the Portuguese he was certainly

under a debt to Rodriguez Lobo's *Corte
na Aldea* (1619), to which he promised
an eternity of fame, and he had read Sá de
Miranda and 'the immortal Camões' (18). 
He must have been acquainted with the
*Ditos da Freira* (1555) of Dona Joana da
Gama, with the *Tempo de Agora* (1622) of
Martim Afonso de Miranda, and especially with the *Imagem da Vida Christam*
(1563, 1572) of Frei Heitor Pinto, who
had made some stir in Spain. Menéndez
y Pelayo drew attention to the close similarity between the opening of *El Criticón*
and that of the *Autodidacto* of Abentofail
(† 1185), while at the same time he
pointed out that the latter work was not
published till twenty years after the first
part of *El Criticón*. In any case the
similarity concerns little more than an ex-
ternal incident, and does not connect *El
Criticón* in the person of Andrenio much
more closely with Abentofail's work than
it is connected in the person of shipwrecked Critilo with Daniel Defoe's
*Robinson Crusoe* (1719).

## IX

BOTH in manner and matter it is to be
feared that Gracián preferred Mateo Alemán or Saavedra Faxardo to Cervantes
and Góngora to Lope de Vega. For him
the first requisite for a writer is point and
acuteness, otherwise his works cannot and
do not deserve to live. According to this
theory the art of Cervantes and Lope de
Vega failed because they did not use their
great gifts with a proper economy; they
lavished themselves without reserving part
of their perfection. The discreet man
must not give himself too fully : *sea un
extremo en la perfección, pero guarde un
medio en el lucimiento.* Gracián was a per-
sistent advocate of the golden mean (the
restraint of excellence, not mediocrity),
and the excesses of genius were as dis-
tasteful to him as the foolish babblings of

the crowd. Not that he placed talent above genius, but he held that no thought could be greatly presented unless it were given a clear and precise setting. The author is thus a lapidary, taking ideas out of the sack of their heavenly existence and fixing them in neat and brilliant sentences. To the *conceptista* the writer who presents ideas in slovenly confusion is as condemnable as those who merely play with words, regardless of ideas. But there is a third pitfall, since the writer, in the belief that he holds an idea may arrange and even torture his words to suit it, while the idea after all escapes, leaving only the unfilled shell of words. Or again the idea may be so ingeniously encased that it is crystallized almost beyond recognition and is with great difficulty connected with the sentence that precedes or follows. There was not to be a superfluous word, in fact verbs and other parts of speech might often be suppressed and a whole thought be condensed into a lonely substantive. Gracián differed from the

*culteranos* in having something to say,
but as a result of this theory of compres-
sion it may be doubted if he will ever
find a very large number of readers.  He
requires the reader's concentrated attention, and as a rule proves himself
worthy of it; sometimes, however, the
nut when cracked is found to be empty,
and then the reader is naturally indignant.
Many passages, indeed the greater part of
*El Criticón* and *El Comulgatorio*, prove
that Gracián could write in a prose which
for clearness and variety has not often
been surpassed and which fascinates
readers by its vigorous simplicity.  To
the question why he did not always so
write many answers might be given.  It is
well to bear in mind the following attri-
bute of his 'discreet' man, as showing
that Gracián was quite capable of wilful
obscurity : 'He should not make his ideas
too easily intelligible.  Most men esteem
that which they do not understand and
admire that which passes their compre-
hension.  A thing must be difficult in

order to be esteemed, and he will be praised when he is not understood.' Moreover there was the prevailing taste of the time which might occasionally mislead even the severest minds and which, to judge from a considerable number of Jesuit writers in Spain and Portugal (one of whom, Antonio Vieira (1608–97), had attained fame as a preacher before Gracián's death), and from splendid churches in which scarcely a square yard is left without ornament, the Jesuits found congenial. Nature in their view required an intellectual heightening, the improvement and adornment provided by art. *No hay belleza sin ayuda*, says Gracián. According to this doctrine the fair flowers of the field would have to be regarded as descendants of artificially cultivated ancestors. It must be remembered, however, that Gracián is chiefly concerned with man. To the question what is beauty? he would probably have answered: keenness. He admits that 'the natural is always more pleasing than the artificial';

he praises, as we have seen, 'natural eloquence', he acknowledges the incomparable beauty of the created world. To the unsophisticated Andrenio the works of God are 'herrlich wie am ersten Tag'. But 'perfection loses by being daily seen'; man's perceptions are soon blunted, and it therefore becomes necessary to stimulate and renew them. 'We pass from life to death without noticing the beauty and perfection of the universe, but the wise turn back and renew their pleasure, contemplating each object with a fresh observation, if not with new sight.' The writer is to effect this renewal for the pleasure and instruction of others. In discussing why the stars were not set in regular lines, 'which would have been a very agreeable sight and a most brilliant artifice', Gracián declares that this arrangement would have been affected and uniform: 'let that be reserved for the toys of art and childish man (*la humana niñería*)'. Men admire things not for their grandeur but for their novelty. What

was yesterday a marvel is to-day despised,
not because it is less perfect but because
men esteem it less, not because it has
changed but because it has not changed
and renewed itself. It is therefore the
function of art to keep on revealing this
unchanging beauty to man by inventing
new modes of expression, new phases and
phrases. 'Wise men by grafting new reflections on old reflections renew the
pleasure through wonder.' Art, he says
in another passage (19), 'is the comple-
ment of Nature, its second being which
beautifies it exceedingly and even claims
to excel it in its works. It boasts to have
added another artificial world to the first.
It usually makes good Nature's short-
comings, perfecting it in everything, since
Nature without the help of this artifice
would remain uncultured and common',
so that 'artifice is the adornment of Nature,
the *realce de su llaneza*'. But since Nature
is very strong, and when turned out with
a pitchfork returns in force (*lo que la horca
destierra con miedo la naturaleza lo revoca*

2285.3

F

*de potencia*), the artist must be ever on the watch and is engaged in an unceasing struggie. The strain on him is twofold, for he must leave no square yard unadorned for Nature to force her way in, and he must also strive persistently to realize his ideal, since ' the works of Nature all come to perfection and then begin to deteriorate, whereas the works of art rarely attain a point at which they cannot be improved '. Since, however, the adorning process must proceed without ceasing, and since *violencias de singularidad* are particularly forbidden, there is an obvious danger of monotony and weariness. In Gracián's style, even apart from such phrases as ' las sedas y damascos fueron ascos ', there are signs of the relentless struggle against the commonplace (20), and it occasionally falls into a surfeit of fanciful conceits.

### X

YET it may plausibly be upheld that the greatest service rendered to Spanish literature by Gracián, keen satirist and ingenious thinker and humorist as he was, consists not in the realm of political or moral thought but, paradoxical as this may appear to those who dismiss him as a decadent or gongorist, in having freed prose style from rhetoric, sluggishness, and superlatives (one of the maxims of the *Oráculo* is *no hablar por superlativos*), and endowed it with an admirable vigour and restraint. According to the Canon of Huesca, who licensed *El Discreto*, Gracián's very commas may have a hidden meaning, and we may accept this in the sense that he paid a most scholarly attention to the form of his sentences. His variety and exuberance are always under strict control. Abroad, where his influence has been mainly exercised (21), it was felt rather as that of a political thinker and moral philosopher. His thought was often betrayed in translation, and a brilliant but somewhat unmethodical thinker might easily become strangely metamorphosed in the hands of French theory or German system. It is improbable that he exercised any marked influence on the thought of Italy—directly, at least: the modernist movement which found expression ultimately in Giuseppe Parini and Vittorio Alfieri came from France (22). It is equally improbable that he influenced John Bunyan, whose *Pilgrim's Progress* was in fact published three years before the English translation of *El Criticón.* *El Criticón* lacks that simple humanity which gives a more fundamental and imposing solemnity to Bunyan's book, making it a work for all mankind, whereas Gracián's great allegory of human life is, in its bitterness, for intellectual man-

kind. Although it was in Germany that
Gracián was most enthusiastically appreciated by the two great philosophers,
Christian Thomasius in the seventeenth
century, Arthur Schopenhauer in the
nineteenth, it was in France and Portugal
that his influence was soonest and perhaps
most deeply felt. The Portuguese were
naturally attracted by an author who spoke
with such sympathetic appreciation of the
Portuguese nation and literature. Mello
probably made sure of meeting the author
of *El Héroe* in 1640, and one likes to
think that Mello's attractive character may
have had something to say to Gracián's
sympathy. Mello's *Apologos Dialogaes*
evidently owe something to *El Criticón*,
especially the third *Apologo*, in which
Boccalini, twice mentioned by Gracián, is
one of the speakers. Later the Jesuit
Alexandre de Gusmão (1695–1753) derived from *El Criticón* the idea of his
*Historia do Predestinado Peregrino y de seu
Irmão Precito*. Neither *El Héroe* nor the
*Oráculo* had appeared in a French form

when Pascal (1623–62), two years before
Gracián's death, wrote the famous *Lettres
provinciales* 'sur la morale et la politique
de ces Pères', but it is permissible to
maintain that Gracián, whom the Jesuit
critic Bouhours (1628–1702) considered
excellent when one could understand him,
influenced moralists such as La Rochefoucauld (1613–80), Saint-Évremond (1613–
1703), and La Bruyère (1645–96) and
even that his doctrines bore fruit in the
philosophers of the eighteenth century and
culminated in the heroic career of Napoleon. Certainly, when Saint-Évremond says
that 'un grand homme ne doit pas laisser
sonder le fonds de sa capacité s'il veut
être toujours admiré du vulgaire'; when
La Bruyère says 'ce n'est pas assez d'avoir
de grandes qualités; il faut en avoir
l'économie', these precepts seem, more
than an echo, a literal translation of
Gracián. Many centuries earlier Hesiod
had affirmed that 'the half is greater than
the whole', a truth which has always pro-
foundly annoyed those to whom it is

meaningless. If the writings of Gracián himself are apt to be unsatisfying, it is not from any lack of intellectual capacity on his part, but perhaps because he fails to realize that man is lord also of the *concepto*, and that human nature may be studied elsewhere than in crowds and cities or in a library. With all his interest in man, there is something a little cold, abstract, and inhuman in his flashing epigrams and paradoxes. Quevedo is more personal, desultory, cynical, and picaresque, even grotesque and brutal, not eschewing *violencias de singularidad*. His laughter is louder, his humour less subtle. Mello is more humane and literary, his method is more historical, his philosophy more practical and social, less concerned with the application of an ideal or Platonic idea. In his truly Spanish *gallardía de espíritu*, to use his own phrase, Gracián was worthy of their friendship, and in all his writings he rises nobly above a dull and sordid materialism. Whether we set him above or on an equality with those two great writers, or, because he gives off an occasional penetrating light from his glittering brilliance rather than a steady human glow of heat, immediately below them, he must always have a prominent place, both as thinker and stylist, in the literature of the seventeenth century and of the world.

## NOTES

(1) Gracianus (= García). In the sixteenth century there was a printer Juan Gracián at Alcalá and the mystic writer Fray Jerónimo Gracián as well as Philip II's secretary.

(2) 'from Zaragoza', says the letter of the General of the Jesuits.

(3) *El Criticón*, Part II, cr. v.

(4) They were published under the name of Lorenzo Gracián. The first part of *El Criticón* appeared under the transparent anagram García de Marlones. The direct personal note is rare in Gracián's work, but in *El Arte de Ingenio* he mentions several of his brothers by name. Lorenzo is not among them, and he may have been a more distant relative, or he may never have existed.

(5) *El Criticón*, Part II, cr. iv.

(6) *Ibid.*, Part III, cr. xii.

(7) Goethe had already written in 1787: 'je mehr ich die Welt sehe, desto weniger kann ich hoffen dass die Menschheit je eine

weise, kluge, glückliche Masse werden könne.'

(8) Eng. tr. London, 1652.

(9) In later editions the order is reversed and the title runs *Agudeza y Arte de Ingenio*. For a criticism of this work see M. Menéndez y Pelayo, *Historia de las Ideas Estéticas en España*, tom. ii, vol. 2 (1884), pp. 535–41 ; also Friedrich Bouterwek, *History of Spanish and Portuguese Literature*, Eng. tr. (1823), vol. i, pp. 536–7.

(10) A. Morel-Fatio in *Bulletin Hispanique*, tom. xii (1910), p. 330.

(11) Eng. tr. J. Jacobs, *The Art of Worldly Wisdom*, London, 1904. No copy of the first (Huesca, 1647) edition of the *Oráculo* is known to exist.

(12) Cf. *El Criticón*, Part III, cr. vi : *El saber bobear es ciencia de ciencias*.

(13) Eng. tr. *Sanctuary Meditations for Priests and Frequent Communicants*, London, 1875.

(14) Eng. tr. *The Critik*, London, 1681.

(15) The *bota* is, of course, the leathern wine-flask—the old bottle of the Scriptures. The *v* in Spanish is pronounced as *b* : *Felices populi quibus vivere est bibere* applies not to the Basques only but to all Spain.

(16) 'Fatal', wrote Richard Ford, 'are those little words *if* and *but* to most Spanish conceptions.'

(17) The English, says Saavedra Faxardo, are grave and severe; the Irish are patient under hardship, despise the arts and boast of the nobility of their descent. The Spanish 'love religion and justice, are constant under adversity, profound in counsel and therefore slow in execution' (cf. Gracián's *lo que le falta al español de prontitud lo suple con el consejo*). They are so haughty that they are not puffed up by prosperity nor humiliated by misfortune. They are the nation which most easily establishes friendly relations with others and most esteems them (*que más bien se da con todas y más las estima*).

(18) *Arte de Ingenio*, ed. 1669, p. 17.

(19) *El Criticón*, Part I, cr. viii.

(20) A bookshop becomes 'one of those shops where learning is marketed'. 'Pourtant', says Professor James Fitzmaurice-Kelly, 'Gracian était supérieur à son œuvre. Observateur avisé et fin, homme d'esprit désillusionné, il est souvent aussi lucide qu'on peut l'être; mais la lucidité ne suffit pas : voulant donner à ses mots plus de signification qu'ils n'en peuvent comporter, Gracian

tombe dans le paradoxe pour éviter le trivial'
(*Littérature Espagnole*, 2^me éd., Paris, 1913,
p. 380).

(21) Narciso José de Liñán y Heredia.
*Baltasar Gracián* (Madrid, 1902), p. 62:
'más apreciado entre los extranjeros que
entre nosotros.' Since these words were
written Señor Martínez Ruiz (Azorín) has devoted a few pages to Gracián in *Lecturas
Españolas* (Madrid, 1912), pp. 65–71, and
Señor Cejador has written his brief but
enthusiastic preface (*El Criticón*, tom. i
(1913), pp. vii–xxiv). Senhor Ricardo Jorge
speaks with keen appreciation of Gracián
(*A sua leitura tem ainda hoje um travo
tonico*) in his remarkable study *Francisco
Rodrigues Lobo* (Coimbra, 1920), pp. 433–4.

(22) *El Criticón* was translated into Italian
in the seventeenth century, *El Héroe, El
Discreto*, and the *Oráculo* in the eighteenth.

# INDEX

PAGES

### A

Abentofail . . . . . . 59
*Agudeza.* See *Arte de Ingenio.*
Alemán (Mateo) . . . . 54, 56, 60
Alfieri (Vittorio) . . . . . 68
Ambrose, Saint . . . . . 25
Arias Montano (Benito) . . . . 56
Ariosto (Lodovico) . . . . . 58
*Arte de Ingenio, El* . 20-3, 57, 73 n., 74 n.
Augustine, Saint . . . . . 25
Azorín, *pseud.* See Martínez Ruiz.

### B

Baltasar Carlos, Prince . . . 57
Boccalini (Traiano) . . . . 58, 69
Borinski (Karl) . . . . . 29
Boscan Almogaver (Juan) . . . 58
Botero (Giovanni) . . . . 58
Bouhours, P. . . . . . 70
Bunyan (John) . . . . 52, 68
Buonarroti (Michelangelo) . . . 11

PAGES

### C

Caesar (Julius) . . . . . . 28
Calderón de la Barca (Pedro) . . . 9
Caligula . . . . . . . 28
Calvin (Jean) . . . . . . 13
Camões (Luis de) . . . . . 59
Castiglione (Baldassare) . . . . 58
Cejador (Julio) . . . . . 76 n.
*Celestina, La* . . . . . . 56
Cervantes (Miguel de) . . . 9, 55, 56, 60
Charles V . . . . . . . 23
*Comulgatorio, El* . . . 7-8, 33-4, 62
Coster (Adolphe) . . . . . 29
*Criticón, El* 2, 6, 35-53, 59, 62, 68, 73 n., 76 n.
Croce (Benedetto) . . . . . 29


### D

Dante Alighieri . . . . . 58
Defoe (Daniel) . . . . . . 59
Diaz (Ruy), el Cid . . . . . 51
*Discreto, El* . . . 26-8, 29, 57, 67, 75 n.


### F

Faret (Nicolas) . . . . . . 26
Farinelli (Arturo) . . . . . 29
Fernando, King, the Catholic . . . 22
Fitzmaurice-Kelly (James) . . . vi, 75 n.
Ford (Richard) . . . . . 75 n.
Fox Morcillo (Sebastian) . . . . 56

PAGES

## G

*Galante, El* . . . . . . . 29
Gama (D. Joana da) . . . . . 59
Goethe (Johann Wolfgang von) . . 73 n.
Góngora (Luis de) . . . . 11, 58
Gracián (Jeronimo) . . . . 73 n.
Gracián (Juan) . . . . . 73 n.
Gracián (Lorenzo) . . . . 73 n.
Gracián y Morales (Baltasar Jerónimo), his birth,
     1 ; education, 1–2 ; Rector of Jesuit College
     at Tarragona, 2 ; punished by his superiors,
     2–3 ; retires to Graus, 3 ; death at Tara-
     zona, 4 ; character and opinions, 5–9 ; pes-
     simism and attitude towards progress, 9–11 ;
     view of democracy, 6, 42 ; his debt to
     Spanish and Portuguese writers, 55–9 ; his
     *conceptismo*, 61–2 ; his conception of Nature,
     63–6 ; his style, 67–8 ; his influence in
     Spain, 67 ; Italy, 68 ; England, 68 ; Ger-
     many, 69 ; France, 69–70 ; Portugal, 69.
Guevara (Antonio de) . . . . 56, 60
Gusmão (Alexandre de) . . . . 69

## H

Henry VIII of England . . . . 51
*Héroe, El* . . . . 20–2, 29, 69, 76 n.
Hesiod . . . . . . . 71
Homer . . . . . . . 58
Horace . . . . . . . 25
Huarte de Sant Juan (Juan) . . . 56

PAGES

I

Isabella, Queen, the Catholic . . 23, 38
Isla (José Francisco de) . . . . 3

J

Jorge (Ricardo) . . . . . 76 n.

L

La Bruyère (Jean de) . . . . . 70
La Rochefoucauld (François de) . . . 70
Lastanosa (Vincencio Juan de) . . . 8
Leon (Luis de) . . . . . 1
Leopardi (Giacomo), Count . . . . 10
Luther (Martin) . . . . . 13

M

Machiavelli (Niccolò) . . . . . 58
Manuel I of Portugal . . . . . 23
Marquez (Juan) . . . . . 56
Martial . . . . . 1, 25, 58
Martínez Ruiz (José) . . . 76 n.
Mello (D. Francisco Manuel de) 1, 2, 34, 69, 71
Menéndez y Pelayo (Marcelino) . 24, 28, 59
Metternich, Prince . . . . 6
Miranda (Martim Afonso de) . . . 59
Morel-Fatio (Alfred) . . . . 29

N

Napoleon I . . . . . 14, 70
Nero . . . . . 28
Nun'Alvarez Pereira . . . . 51

PAGES

O

*Oráculo Manual* 28–33, 35, 67, 69, 74 n., 76 n.

P

Parini (Giuseppe) . . . . . . 68
Pascal (Blaise) . . . . . . 70
Pérez de Vargas (Diego) . . . . 22
Petrarca (Francesco) . . . . . 58
Philip II of Spain . . . . . 22
Pinto (Heitor) . . . . . . 59
Plato . . . . . . . 40, 55
*Político, El* . . . . . . 22–3

Q

Quevedo y Villegas (Francisco Gómez de)
1, 9, 11, 34, 57, 71

R

Rivadeneyra (Pedro de) . . . . 56
Rodriguez Lobo (Francisco) . . . 59
Roland . . . . . . . 51
Romulus . . . . . . . 23

S

Saavedra Faxardo (Diego) . . 57, 60, 75 n.
Sá de Miranda (Francisco de) . . . 59
Saint-Évremond (Charles de Saint-Denys de) 70
Salazar (Ambrosio de) . . . . 26
Sanchez (Francisco) . . . . 56
Schopenhauer (Arthur) . . . 10, 29, 69
*Selvas del Año* . . . . . 34
Seneca . . . . 40, 41, 54, 55

AND MONOGRAPHS III

PAGES

**T**

Tacitus . . . . . . . 58
Tasso (Torquato) . . . . . 58
Teresa, Santa . . . . . . 30
Theotocopuli (Domenico) el Greco . 57
Thomasius (Christian) . . . . 69
Timanthes . . . . . . 57
Titian . . . . . . . 11

**V**

*Varón Atento, El* . . . . . 29
Vega Carpio (Lope Felix de) . . 9, 60
Velazquez (Diego) . . . . . 57
Vieira (Antonio) . . . . . 63
Virgil . . . . . . . 58
Vives (Juan Luis) . . . . . 56

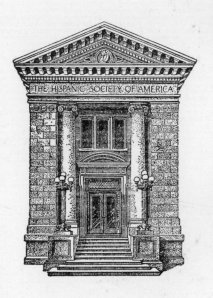